TOY TRAINS

Bob Leggett

SHIRE PUBLICATIONS
Bloomsbury Publishing Plc
PO Box 883, Oxford, OX1 9PL, UK
1385 Broadway, 5th Floor, New York, NY 10018, USA

E-mail: shire@bloomsbury.com
www.shirebooks.co.uk

SHIRE is a trademark of Osprey Publishing Ltd

First published in Great Britain in 2019

ISBN: PB 978 1 78442 308 7
eBook 978 1 78442 309 4
ePDF 978 1 78442 310 0
XML 978 1 78442 307 0

19 20 21 22 23   10 9 8 7 6 5 4 3 2 1

Typeset by PDQ Digital Media Solutions, Bungay, UK

Printed and bound in India by Replika Press Private Ltd.

Shire Publications supports the Woodland Trust, the UK's leading woodland conservation charity.

COVER IMAGE
Front cover: The mid-1950s all-metal Hornby Dublo 3-rail 'Duchess of Atholl' Passenger set and the mid-1960s Tri-ang Hornby plastic-bodied Jinty and Car Transporter from the popular Car-a-Belle Train Set. (Deborah Rosenthal)

Back cover: The iconic 'Princess' bursting out of the Train set box was marketed by Rovex in 1951 for Marks and Spencer. (Tony Blackman)

TITLE PAGE IMAGE
Tri-ang Railways' beautifully detailed 'Lord of the Isles' Train Set.

CONTENTS PAGE IMAGE
Hornby Dublo's Sir Nigel Gresley LNER electric passenger set with articulated tinplate coaches, complete with transformer.

ACKNOWLEDGEMENTS
Images are gratefully acknowledged as follows:

Author, pages 4, 10, 11, 17 (bottom), 22 (top), 35, 40 (top), 41 (top), 42 (top left), 42 (top right), 48 (bottom), 50, 57; Brian Salter, page 13 (bottom); Chris Graebe, pages 3, 15 (top), 15 (bottom), 16, 17 (top); David O'Brien, pages 12 (top), 12 (bottom), 13 (top), 29 (top), 29 (bottom); Paul Catchpole/ World of Model Railways, Mevagissey, page 59; Michael Bowes, page 20 (top); National Motor Museum Beaulieu, page 58; Richard Lines, pages 17 (top), 34. All other images are courtesy of Deborah Rosenthal.

The author would like to thank all those who have given support, encouragement and advice. Also to those who continue to 'play trains' and give pleasure with their vintage layouts at shows up and down the country.

CONTENTS

FOREWORD

I was delighted when Bob advised me he was writin
about the history of pre- and post-war 00 gauge toy train
This gauge has often been scantily covered in the variou
books on the history of toy trains.

Bob has explained what 00 gauge is and why it becam
the most popular gauge. He gives an insight into the excitir
times in post-war Britain as the economy recovered from th
devastation of the war.

Richard Lines
(right) with the
author in 2018.

I was fortunate to be part of the Tri-ang Group that helped create the golden age of 00 gauge toy trains in the late 1950s and early 1960s, which gave so much joy to boys and girls.

Technology has now advanced, with finely produced models, mainly from the Far East. Digital operation has the models operating like the railways of today, so it is encouraging to know that there is still a large group of enthusiasts who enjoy playing with their original toy trains. Long may it last. Thank you, Bob, for bringing back some wonderful memories.

Richard Lines
September 2018

The author's well-played-with Defender set, complete with added camouflage. (See page 37)

INTRODUCTION

THIS BOOK TELLS the story of RTR (ready to run 00 gauge toy trains in the UK from 1936, when Tri: launched its HO/00 gauge system in the UK, until 1975. have not included the modelling area of 00 gauge such as fine locomotive and rolling stock kits and other fine modelling accessories, although popular manufacturers with accessorie for the masses have been included.

By nature of the subject, the detail about each manufacture is quite limited, although Rovex (who made Tri-ang Railways fills more space than most as it was the dominant manufacture from 1955 to 1975. There are several books written abou the concise history of most of the manufacturers of 00 gaug trains, and I have given a list at the end of this book. I woulc also like to thank all the authors who put so much time int their books and on the internet, some of whom have gladl helped me with information for this book.

Today 00 gauge is unique to the UK. Although the tracl width is the same as HO (half 0) gauge (16.5mm), the siz of the models is to a scale of 1:72, whereas the actual scale should be smaller at 1:87, the correct scale for 16.5mn track, i.e. HO gauge.

The main reason for the discrepancy emerged in th formative days of 00 gauge, when the bodies of locomotive were enlarged to fit firstly clockwork and later electric motors Even Marklin in Germany started in 1936 with 00 gaug before moving to HO after the war.

Technology soon developed, and continental European and American firms adapted their models to the correct scale of 1:87. In the UK, however, Trix's 1936 HO/00 gauge was closely followed by Meccano's Hornby Dublo, which entered the market in 1938 with a constant 00 scale. Other British manufacturers followed suit, and as a result the UK stands alone with 00 gauge.

During the period 1955–70, the British economy was buoyant. In July 1957, Prime Minister Harold MacMillan, said in his speech at a Conservative rally in Bedford, 'most of our people have never had it so good'. Britain had recovered from the Second World War and was just about to start the swinging sixties. A train set was on most boys' Christmas list in this period, and the manufacturers filled their stockings with glee.

This history of 00 gauge toy trains ends in 1975, as this was the year when manufacturing of 00 gauge trains for the British market first moved to the Far East. This commenced when the well-known kit maker Airfix entered the RTR market and had its models produced in Hong Kong. These models had much greater detail than the main UK manufacturer, Hornby Railways, and by using significantly lower labour costs they were considerably cheaper, becoming more model-like. For these reasons, 1975 can be seen as being the beginning of the end of the toy 00 gauge railway.

Examples of locomotives of various gauges (from front to back): O Gauge Tri-ang Hymek diesel; 00 Gauge Tri-ang AIA AIA diesel; HO Gauge Lima Class 33 diesel; TT Gauge Tri-ang AIA AIA diesel; 000/N Gauge Lone Star American diesel.

MINIATURE TABLE RAILWAY.

THE BEGINNING TO 1945

MODEL RAILWAYS AND toy trains go back to Victorian times, when prosperous families were able to commission models directly from craftsmen and engineers and eventually from toy manufacturers, particularly in Germany from companies such as Marklin and Bing.

However, these models were generally large scale, from 0 gauge to gauge 3 and even larger, and very expensive. They were propelled mainly by clockwork or steam, as electric technology was not developed fully until the twentieth century. The buyers of these expensive models were generally the gentry of the day, who would have lived in substantial town and city dwellings into which large rooms and gardens the toy and model trains would easily have fitted.

Up until the First World War this was generally the case with most models made by German companies, many sold through the well-known British company Bassett-Lowke.

After the initial austerity following the First World War, there was a huge house-building programme in the 1920s and 30s, with 'Metro-land' in the south and other large suburban areas being created across the UK. There was a rise in the middle class 'white collar' workers who commuted to London and other cities, whose income was beginning to allow greater expenditure on toys, with Christmas and birthdays becoming more popular for present-giving to children.

The problem with toy and model trains in this context was their size. The new houses were much smaller and could not

OPPOSITE
1920s Bing 00 gauge clockwork table top train set in LMS livery produced in Germany for the British market.

A Victorian train, c.1870s, in a reconstruction of a nursery – it was probably only allowed to be played with on a Sunday, hence the excellent condition.

accommodate the large-scale trains and other toys that were comfortably played with in the substantial nursery rooms of the Victorian and Edwardian mansions.

Companies therefore looked at building smaller train sets. In the 1920s the famous German toy maker Bing launched a new, smaller train set entitled Bing Table Top. This was approximately half 0 gauge (HO), and is widely regarded as the first smaller system made to approximately 00 scale. Almost everything was made of tin, and Bing managed to produce a fine system including locomotives, rolling stock, stations, bridges, tunnels and other items. This was a remarkable feat, as Bing used the latest technology and was able for the first time to fit both clockwork and electric motors into the small engine bodies. Clockwork remained a popular choice as mains electricity was still not available in many households. The Europeans named the smaller gauge 'HO' (half 0).

Bing was soon followed by the French company JEP Mignon, which launched a similar system with overhead catenary. Both of these had moderate success, but despite the smaller sizes neither system lasted and were discontinued by the early 1930s.

Despite the great economic crash at the end of the 1920s and the austerity of the early 1930s, those who had jobs prospered, as mentioned in Kenneth Brown's book *The British Toy Industry*. The cost of food was greatly reduced and families were able to increase their spending on non-essentials. Such availability of money to those with smaller housing created a demand for a smaller gauge and both Meccano and Trix introduced 00 gauge. This time it was here to stay.

JEP Mignon's 1920s short-lived tinplate 00 gauge locomotive, the first 00 gauge system to use overhead catenary.

TRIX AND HORNBY LAUNCH 00 GAUGE

TRIX

In 1935 Stephan Bing, who had helped launch Bing Table Top in the 1920s, joined with Siegfried Kahn to produce a new comprehensive 00/HO gauge system called Trix Express in Germany. Setting their sights high, they developed excellent die-cast locomotives, a large range of rolling stock and a robust 3-rail track with Bakelite base and the ability to run two trains on one track at the same time by using each outer rail with the centre rail.

Bassett-Lowke, which was a well-known distributor of 0 gauge and larger model railways as well as steam boats, waterline models and other models for mostly affluent customers, had had dealings with Bing in the past and saw the possibilities of the new gauge. It jointly helped launch Trix Twin (as it was initially known) at the 1936 British Industries Fair in the UK. It was actually very confusing at the beginning as Trix called its system Trix Express and Bassett-Lowke marketed it as Twin Trains.

Impressive locomotives were produced, such as the 'Flying Scotsman' with LNER (London and North Eastern Railway) coaches, 'Princess' with LMS (London, Midland and Scottish

Railway) coaches, and the cream of the locomotives, a streamline Coronation class based on the 'Royal Scot' locomotive with matching maroon coaches. Presented in special presentation boxes, these sets were praised by the model railway press and the magazines of the day, heralding the birth of 00 gauge in the UK.

Trix also impressed with its wonderful 'manyways' station, originally in wood and later in metal, which could be configured as a terminus or through station and had an iconic Art Deco style. It was a very robust system that lasted for many years in the Trix catalogues

The peak of Trix's pre-war 00 gauge manufacturing was its wonderful LMS pre-war 'Coronation' set with the streamline locomotive and matching coaches.

Trix also developed a fine collection of wooden buildings, including signal boxes, engine sheds, goods depot and other lineside buildings. It had initially satisfied the north with its fine steam locomotives from that region and to show no favouritism produced a Portsmouth Southern Electric EMU (electric multiple unit), which was probably its first actual 00 gauge model. With wonderful artwork on the lid, this immediately appealed to Southern fans.

Trix rapidly expanded its system and was assisted by Britains (which had close links to Trix), the well-known lead figure

Mid-1930s Trix Express 00 gauge locomotive and tender, which helped start the new wave of 00 gauge trains.

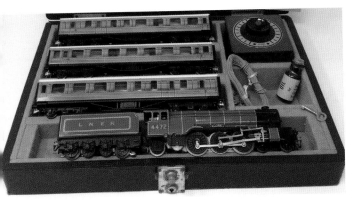

The superb Trix pre-war 00 gauge 'Flying Scotsman' and LNER 'Teak'-style coaches set in its attractive presentation box.

and animal manufacturer, which launched its Lilliput range of accessories for 00 Gauge model railways. By the beginning of the Second World War, Trix had a comprehensive 00 gauge system that was well received by the public and was ready for expansion after the war.

Trix was not the only German company to launch 00 gauge. In 1937 Marklin also produced LMS and LNER passenger sets and a compound 4-4-0 locomotive for the UK market, but it did not develop the system and after the war it concentrated on Continental HO gauge.

HORNBY DUBLO

Hornby, part of the Meccano group, had pioneered its 0 gauge system in the early 1920s. By the late 1930s it was producing some wonderful 0 gauge locomotives, epitomised by the superb LMS 'Princess Elizabeth' locomotive, which was issued in 1937.

Meccano had also noticed the Trix development and was fully aware of the huge social and economic changes that were happening in the UK.

A busy scene at the entrance to Trix's iconic 1930s Art Deco 'manyways' station building, which was manufactured into the 1960s.

Hornby's 0 gauge masterpiece, the superb 'Princess Elizabeth'.

By the mid-1930s it was discussing launching a 00 gauge (Dublo) system and was no doubt frustrated when Trix beat them to it, as a result initially losing out on a significant customer base.

When Meccano was ready to introduce Hornby Dublo it was able to launch the new system to its well-established network of retail customers that had shops (agents) in most towns and cities in the UK, most of whom were tied to Meccano, which had a policy of only one agent per town. Although good news for the agent, this was later to backfire on Meccano when Tri-ang Railways was launched after the war with fewer restrictions on who could sell its toys.

Meccano magazine, with its perenially eye-catching covers, was a must for train and model enthusiasts from the 1930s to the 1970s.

Meccano also had another very strong weapon, *Meccano* magazine. This magazine, although titled *Meccano*, was in fact a wonderful monthly journal that covered all subjects such as Hornby 0 gauge trains, Meccano, Hornby boats, Dinky toys and all sorts of fascinating information and stories usually related to air, sea or land transportation. The magazine was instrumental in setting up Meccano and Hornby clubs at many schools. In the 1930s, circulation was approximately 70,000 and Meccano was able to launch Hornby Dublo via the magazine and their agents to a captive audience.

Being a large company that had survived the economic crash intact in the late 1920s and the subsequent depression of the early 1930s, with

ts network of agents Meccano was
deally placed to hit the new market of
middle-class suburbia and an affluent
working class that were being created
by the huge house-building schemes
of the 1930s. Even the Metropolitan
Railway was building mock Tudor
emi-detached houses to complement
ts new line from Farrington.

 With great fanfare, Meccano launched Dublo in 1937 with
both electric and clockwork power. Initially, it produced an
excellent passenger train set comprising a Gresley A4 in LNER
blue named 'Sir Nigel Gresley', with teak-style articulated
coaches, track and transformer, and a goods set comprising an
0-6-2T N2 tank locomotive in either LNER or LMS liveries
with three trucks, track and transformer (with GWR [Great
Western Railway] and SR [Southern Railway] liveries appearing
ater). Both engines were available in clockwork or electric with
wo types of track, 3-rail for the electric and 2-rail for clockwork.

 Hornby Dublo matched Trix and produced a superb
wooden canopy terminus/through station as well as a suburban

This pre-war
advert for the
newly launched
Hornby Dublo
trains shows how
much could be
achieved on the
dining table, if
Mum allowed!

Hornby Dublo
pre-war rare
Southern
clockwork
goods set.

station, island platform, goods depots and signal boxes all in wood, most initially with red roofs and latterly with green roofs. In addition, an excellent 2-road engine shed and metal signals both manual and electric were introduced. Dinky Toys, which was also owned by Meccano, produced toy vehicles and figures to complement the new Dublo system.

The superb Hornby Dublo City Station set, which could be set up as a terminus or through station.

Dublo was a 3-rail system that only allowed one engine to operate on the track at a time, unlike the Trix Twin system. Nevertheless, with the *Meccano* magazine and the large network of retail shops supporting the Meccano group, the system was successfully launched in 1938 and grew rapidly until Britain and Germany commenced hostilities in September 1939.

THE SECOND WORLD WAR: HUGAR

The war years 1939–45 were, not surprisingly, unkind to toy manufacturers, particularly those that produced metal toys. In the early months of the war the toy market was hardly affected, but as Germany and its Axis partners captured more and more of Europe it was evident there would be restrictions upon metal toys in Britain. Various war acts were passed restricting the use of metal in toys and, by 30 September 1943, the sale of all metal models or toys was banned, whether new, complete, in parts or second-hand. The Meccano factory was converted to produce munitions for the war effort, and down in the south, Tri-ang, the largest toy company in the world, was producing machine guns and other items for the war effort in their huge Merton factory.

However, one manufacturer, Hugar, who produced wooden scenic accessories before the war, tried to fill the gap left by Hornby Dublo and Trix by producing a Southern Electric model railway set, predominantly using wooden

omponents. The driving coach
nd bodies were made of solid
vood with paper sides with a metal
notorised bogie, the track was also
olid wood with metal rails set into
. This was almost certainly the last
ew toy train built during the war
nd was available until the 1943
netal toy ban. Due to wartime
estrictions the quality of this
nodel was poor, and it is no wonder that this set did not
erform very well. Despite the wartime demand for toys,
nany remained unsold. We are fortunate today that Paul
rookes, a member of the Train Collectors Society, has been
lifelong Hugar collector and has been able to source and
un these models at shows around the country.

From Sept 1943, those companies who had the resources were
ft to produce scratch-built models with whatever non-metal
naterials they could get hold of. Restrictions were lifted towards
ne end of the war, although materials were still hard to find.

The Tri-ang
Merton Factory
produced
millions of
items for the
war effort.
Here is part of
a glider being
manufactured for
D-Day.

HUGAR
MODEL TRAIN

"SOUTHERN ELECTRIC"
"00" GAUGE SCALE MODEL ELECTRIC TRAIN SET

One of the few
sets produced
during the war
was the Hugar 00
gauge Southern
Electric train
set, produced
mainly in wood,
including the
track.

POST WAR AUSTERITY: SMALLER COMPANIES

Despite Britain and its Allies winning the Second World War, the country was basically broke. Many cities were severely bomb-damaged and a large workforce was therefore involved in rebuilding the infrastructure. The government was keen to encourage all major manufacturing companies to help an export drive that would bring money into the UK. This made the large toy manufacturers slow to progress in the UK's domestic model railway market.

On the plus side, there was for a short while a metal surplus, as it was no longer required for the war effort. Back from the war were many engineers and entrepreneurs seeking ways to use their skills and hopefully make money from new start-up businesses. As a result, there was a glut of manufacturers who tried their hand producing toys, including 00 gauge trains.

Mettoy and Brimtoy were well known pre- and post-Second World War toy manufacturers including O gauge toy trains. They both entered the 00 gauge market. Copying their large models, these were very toy-like and aimed at the younger enthusiast. They initially used tinplate track similar to 0 gauge track. Mettoy actually hit the market with its first 00 gauge sets in 1939, although little is known of this set. Post-war, Mettoy continued to produce both 0 gauge and 00 gauge play sets. The 00 sets included a 4-wheel Battle of Britain locomotive 'Spitfire', with either a circle of track or a solid base shunting game. The set came with two coaches and tinplate track.

OPPOSITE
Pyramid Toys Trackmaster clockwork train set, which was to become part of the original Tri-ang Railways system.

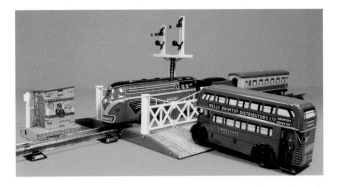

Wells Brimtoy 00 Gauge trains and accessories were very colourful, although they were not compatible with Hornby Dublo, Trix or Tri-ang.

Brimtoy produced its first 00 gauge set after the war which again was very toy-like. They did however, produce an electric passenger set and a BR-type diesel locomotive goods set with battery-powered controllers. Mainly sold through outlets such as Woolworths these sets sold quite well but were not compatible with Trix or Hornby Dublo systems, and Brimtoy did not expand the range beyond the sets and a few tinplate accessories. Brimtoy later produced cheap plastic clockwork sets compatible with Tri-ang, which sold fairly well in Woolworths, smaller toy shops and corner shops.

Ever Ready were well known for their battery and cycle lamps, but were keen to produce electronic toys that had use for their batteries. Many homes were still using accumulators for their radios as mains electricity was still not widely available. They looked outside the box and in 1950 produced a rather fetching Underground set based on a Bakerloo Line unit. Using aluminium, which at the time was widely available as it had been produced in large quantities for Spitfires, this was an attractive product that was well advertised, and it sold

Gaiety Toys, also known as Castle Art, were based in Birmingham and produced a clockwork 0-6-2T and 0-6-0 Pannier tank.

n good numbers. As with Hugar, enthusiasts are still running these trains today, although metal fatigue affects the wheels and parts of the motors due to weak alloys. Collectors often replace the bogie with a modern model.

Champion Products Ltd from Birmingham produced a rather bulbous Champion Flyer rail car electric 2-rail set in 1948. This was followed up by an improved model. However, this was the extent of their range.

Ever Ready's notable London Underground set, produced from surplus aluminium from the Second World War.

Scalemaster models, built by Electric Toys Ltd, around 1949 produced a futuristic streamline locomotive and tender in several colours with a set of coaches and track. Little else is known about this manufacturer and the model's production run.

Exley were well known for their 0 gauge coaches, but they also produced a very pleasing electric-powered 00 gauge SR EMU set and a variety of coaches.

Graham Farish possibly introduced the first 2-rail 00 gauge system in 1949. This was quite a significant move. Initially, a metal 3-rail black 0-6-0 locomotive and tender was produced, rather similar to a Southern Q class. With 4 trucks and an oval of 3-rail track, a very pleasing set, produced in their Bromley factory. Graham Farish went on to produce a selection of 2-rail locomotives, including a well-made Merchant Navy Class locomotive, King Edward 4-6-0, Saddle Tank and an 0-6-2 tank based on GWR design. Coaches could be purchased in RTR or kit form. They produced full-length Pullman cars in acetate (an early

The Champion Flyer, featuring a possible link with Ever Ready.

Graham Farish's excellent Merchant Navy Class locomotive and tender 'Port Line', resplendent in early BR blue livery.

form of plastic). Unfortunately, little was known about the properties of some early plastics, and many of the acetate models suffered from warping within quite a short period after production.

Unfortunately, Graham Farish did not fine-tune their system, which used a two-pole motor with an awkward connection from tender to loco to drive the locomotive. They lost out against the choice and running quality available from Hornby Dublo. Although they continued to dip into the 00 gauge market, they never acquired a strong foothold.

In the late 1940s, **Pyramid Toys** produced a very pleasing train set using an 0-6-2 metal tank locomotive with a powerful clockwork drive and several plastic trucks on a 2-rail metal track. This was marketed under the name of Trackmaster and sold in excellent numbers.

Rovex was the brainchild of George Vanetzian, a toy maker in the late 1940s, who was keen to use the new types of plastic. Not only were they cheaper than metal, but they were easier for creating detailed moulds and could produce more items very quickly. His vision was to produce a significant train set for the new post-war market. He was already producing plastic toys under the name of Rovex and had had several successful contracts supplying these toys to Marks and Spencer (M&S) at Christmas. For Christmas 1950, M&S

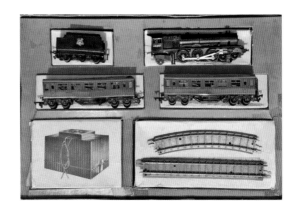

ad asked if it was possible o produce an 00 gauge train et, as they felt there was a demand for toy trains. Not one to do things lightly, instead of manufacturing an easy tank engine and trucks he decided to build a Princess 4-6-2 locomotive and tender in plastic using a Zenith motor, plastic wheels and a roller pick-up on realistic 2-rail ballasted track, with two coaches.

Rovex train set with a later-issue 'Princess Elizabeth' using plunger pick-ups.

The set he produced looked brilliant and was immediately in high demand. M&S were of course delighted with the set. However, due to issues with the roller pick-up collecting fluff, which greatly reduced the effectiveness of the model, there were constant changes required to produce a better engine and he was not able to produce enough sets to meet his contractual commitment. He was therefore delighted when one of the major toy companies was interested in buying his company (see page 33).

Anbrico and Kirdon: both these companies were really aiming their products in the 1950s and early 1960s at the modeller. However, they both produced a small quality range of RTR diesel locomotives and railcars.

In the 1950s BR was replacing aged stock with cost-effective railcars, and this RTR example by Kirdon was an excellent representation.

POST-WAR HORNBY DUBLO AND TRIX

HORNBY DUBLO

Early post-war 'Duchess of Atholl' passenger train set by Hornby Dublo.

Meccano was quite slow to recover after the war. The company was also not helped by the government insisting on producing items for the export market to help the economy recover. The home market was desperate for new trains, but Dinky Toys and Meccano had to wait until the late 1940s for the full range to be available in the UK.

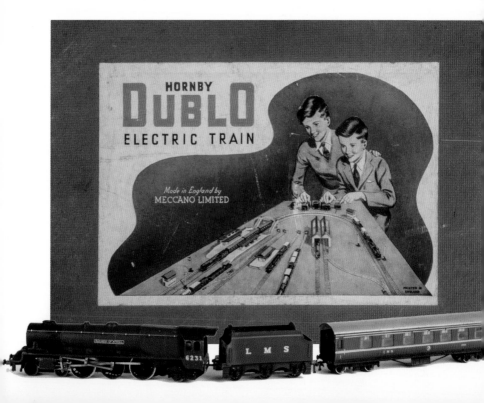

The death of Frank Hornby in 1936 was a big blow to Meccano. His son Roland was not of the same mould as his father and Meccano was generally less imaginative and forward-thinking post-war, relying on its pre-war reputation.

However, the cessation of toy making in 1943 left Meccano with hundreds of thousands of pre-war parts for 0 and 00 gauge trains, Meccano and Dinky toys. Initially, many post-war toys included pre-war parts. Meccano was also aware of the demographic changes affecting the UK and decided, perhaps prematurely, to dramatically reduce its excellent near-scale Hornby 0 gauge trains to only toy trains with 4-wheel tender and tank clockwork locomotives and rolling stock, apart from a few larger export models.

The opposite was the case for Hornby Dublo Trains. this was their main focus, but they made one big error in that they dropped the clockwork trains. It is unclear why, but this was certainly a big mistake as they had no entry-level train sets to encourage the younger train enthusiast. In 1952, when Tri-ang launched its system, several clockwork trains sets were on offer for the younger enthusiast. Hornby did not produce wooden buildings after the war and delayed introducing its range of aluminium buildings, which included a station, island platform and signal box, until the early 1950s, sadly without an engine shed or goods depot.

Thus, Dublo concentrated on the electric range and, with the help of *Meccano magazine* and the company's agents, got back up and running. There is no doubt that Dublo locomotives and rolling stock

The new BR lined black livery 0-6-2T produced by Dublo following nationalisation of the railways in 1948.

were very well made, solidly engineered and reliable, although a little expensive. Dublo was, however, a little slow to adapt to the new livery when BR was formed in 1948, eventually replacing all their pre-nationalisation stock with BR livery by the early 1950s.

Dublo also never went back to using the liveries of the previous 'Big Four' railway companies, GWR, LMS, LNER and SR. This was another error, as they missed giving enthusiasts the opportunity to purchase locos and coaches in other liveries. Its tinplate trucks and coaches were also beginning to look dated against the new colourful and cheaper plastic-moulded stock from Tri-ang and Trix.

Hornby Dublo slowly moved into the 1960s, having being overtaken on sales by Tri-ang by the late 1950s. It was not until 1959 that it launched its 2-rail track system. It also introduced its 'superdetail' stock, which was a revelation; even by today's standards, the fine tinplate finish with flush glazing on the coaches is considered second to none. They also brought out a superb range of plastic buildings, including a well-regarded through/terminus station, station, engine shed and goods depot.

A range of excellent Dublo Dinky toys was also produced, and new locomotives such as the E3002 were appearing.

Dublo even produced some attractive starter sets,

Hornby Dublo's attempt to encourage their export market with a fairly basic alteration of the Duchess locomotive to represent a Canadian example and conversion of the Brake van to a Caboose.

The new Dublo 'super detailed' stock was a sensation. This is the rare 6-wheel 'Stove' passenger brake van.

Dublo's excellent rebuilt West Country-class locomotive and tender 'Barnstaple'.

Dublo produced this very attractive EMU in Southern green livery in the early 1960s.

One of the last projects by Dublo was this very simple track cleaning car.

but sadly, as the company was supporting both 2- and 3-rail sets, and since sales were not sufficient and other areas of the Meccano business were struggling with competition, it eventually went into administration and sold out to the Lines Group (Tri-ang).

Tri-ang incorporated several of the Hornby models into its own range and even produced the through/terminus station in Tri-ang maroon. As it turned out, Wrenn's later acquisition of the moulds kept the Dublo models going longer than their original time under Meccano!

Dinky Toys catalogue showing part of the range of Dublo Dinky Toys that complemented the Hornby Dublo system.

DUBLO *DINKY TOYS*

Dublo Dinky Toys are made to the scale of 'OO' gauge trains
They add much to the realism and fun of model railway working

062
Singer Roadster
Length 2"   1/6

063
Commer Van
Length 2¼"   1/6

064
Austin Lorry
Length 2½"   1/6

067
Austin Taxi
Length 2⁷⁄₁₆"   2/5

068
Royal Mail Van (with windows)
Length 1⅞"   2/2

069
Massey-Harris-Ferguson Tractor
Length 1⁷⁄₈"   1/6

All prices in this booklet include Purchase Tax

Dublo screw-together plastic kit of the early 1960s, including a much-admired 5083 terminus or through station kit that also came with extension kits.

TRIX

Trix was another company that did not fare well after the war. Obviously, being German did not help. The magnificent locomotives produced pre-war did not rematerialise and Trix concentrated mainly on fairly simple 0-4-0 tanks, tender locomotives and European outline diesel railcars. Although the buildings remained in the range with their set of accessories, Trix was expensive and looking second rate with the dated 3-rail track.

Trix also went through many financial difficulties in the 1950s and 1960s, but nevertheless produced some excellent die-cast locomotives in the late 1950s, including an 0-6-2 tank, Britannia locomotive and Warship class diesel.

By the early 1960s Trix was owned by the Courtalds group and was producing an excellent range of plastic-bodied locomotives, including the LNER 'Flying Scotsman' with two tenders, 'A H Peppercorn', A4 locomotives and a Trans-Pennine Railcar DMU, and coaches, although the coaches were made more to HO gauge than 00 gauge, which restricted sales.

A good range of wagons was also produced. However, financially Trix was always looking over its shoulder, and was never able to rekindle the pre-war success of its system.

A pair of Trix Standard Class 4-6-0 locomotives with die-cast bodies and tenders issued in the mid-1950s. These quality models could at last compete with Hornby Dublo and Tri-ang.

In the early 1960s Trix produced plastic-bodied locomotives with superb detail. Here is the excellent Class A2 'A H Peppercorn' in BR green.

LOCAL PASSENGER TRAIN SET

PULLMAN TRAIN SET

CRASH TRAIN SET

HIGHWAYMAN TRAIN SET

FRONTIERSMAN TRAIN SET

SNOW RESCUE TRAIN

THE GIANT AWAKES: ENTER TRI-ANG

IN 1939 TRI-ANG was the largest toy company in the world, with various factories in the UK. The main factory was in Merton, South London, which eventually became the largest toy factory in the world. Tri-ang had purchased Hamleys toy shop in Regent Street, London in 1931 to push their products to the affluent London and tourist markets. At this time Hamleys was probably the most famous toy shop in the world. Tri-ang also supported a huge network of toy shops selling its goods across the UK as well as the countries that formed part of the British Empire, including Canada, Australia, New Zealand and South Africa.

Despite being a prolific maker of pedal cars, castles, garages, bicycles, scooters, dolls' houses, dolls, prams, push chairs, play shops and many, many other toys, Tri-ang did not produce a toy train system.

It may seem surprising that Tri-ang had not followed Hornby and Chad Valley and other British manufacturers into the 0 gauge market in the 1920s, but it was very successful at producing a huge variety of wood and steel toys, keeping its factories at full production.

Richard Lines, son of Arthur Lines (one of the three founders of the Lines group which became Tri-ang Toys) became a director of the company after the Second World War. He believes there was no reason for Tri-ang to have entered the 0 gauge market, but tells a very interesting story. In the early 1930s, the British government was worried that German toy

OPPOSITE
A shop poster supplied by Tri-ang showing the wonderful range of action sets available in 1963.

makers were too successful in the UK, particularly with thei
toy trains and other tin toys. Tri-ang and possibly Meccanc
received visits from the Ministry of Trade and pressure wa
placed upon them to produce more toys, particularly trains
The relationship between the two companies at this time wa
very respectful, and Richard held Frank Hornby in very higl
esteem. Since Hornby was well established in the toy trair
market, there was no point causing conflict with Meccano anc
competing with them. However, Tri-ang took the governmen
request very seriously and even sent one of the Lines' cousin.
to work in a German factory to find the secret of the Germar
toy market! Instead of producing train sets, Tri-ang producec
a new range of Minic tinplate clockwork toy vehicles
These became hugely popular and were great sellers, ever
complementing the Hornby 0 gauge railway system. Hornb
also expanded its 0 gauge range in the 1930s and launchec
Dublo (as we have read) in 1938, so it appears both companie
took on board the government's wishes.

Just before the Second World War the Lines Brothers boarc
no doubt discussed the success Trix and Hornby had entering
the market for 00 gauge trains. However, the economy wa:
good in pre-war Britain and in 1937 Tri-ang was flat ou
meeting huge demands for their large selection of toys. Tri-ang
was not producing die-cast toys, which would have been ar
expensive divergence, and plastic was still being developed.

With the outbreak of war, Triang's toy production dic
not last long, and its factories were applied to the war effort
The Tri-ang factory in Merton, South London was heavily
bombed in the summer of 1940, but this did not stop i
producing over one million machine guns; fourteen millior
magazines; thousands of magazines for Spitfire and Hurricanc
fighters; millions of shell cases; 3,500 model aircraft for targe
purposes; and fuselages for 32-foot wingspan gliders. Thei
experimental department even produced scale models of the
Normandy beaches for D-Day.

At the end of the Second World War, Tri-ang began to rebuild its toy empire – a difficult task for the larger manufacturers as they had to retool their factories and start producing high quality toys again. Around summer 1951, one of the Tri-ang directors, Alan Cathcart, who was general manager of the doll department, spotted the Rovex Princess set in an M&S store. On sale for 59s 6d, he purchased it and took it back to Merton to show Walter Lines, chairman of the Lines Group, stating that they could do something with it.

Walter Lines had a reputation that when he liked something he made sure it was pushed through. He was so impressed with the Rovex train set, which was produced mainly in plastic, that he arranged a meeting with Mr Vanetzian, the MD of Rovex. Quite soon they discovered Rovex (which also owned Zenith, the electric motor manufacturer for the Princess locomotive) was struggling to meet its contractual commitment to M&S. Rovex eventually delivered 45,000 sets (three quarters of their original contract), mainly due to lack of brass for motors created by the severe restrictions on non-ferrous metals by the Korean War.

Mr Vanetzian was probably delighted that Tri-ang was in the market to buy his company. Walter personally interviewed the six members of the Rovex board and took them all on. They included John Hefford, who had come with Zenith. Richard Lines advised Tri-ang to continue to use the name Rovex until it was happy with the quality of the finished product. In January 1952, Tri-ang had to employ a group of workers to repair the large numbers of faulty Rovex Princesses returned to the factory.

The original Rovex 'Princess Elizabeth' passenger train set, with the inefficient roller pick-ups under the cab. Note also the warping of the early acetate plastic coaches.

Tri-ang was also impressed with Pyramid Toys, whic produced the Trackmaster 00 gauge clockwork train se which consisted of a die-cast 00 gauge 0-6-2 tank engine (ver similar to the Hornby Dublo model engine), plastic truck with metal chassis and an oval of solid metal track (no points It was a very well-made set with a good clockwork moto However, unsurprisingly, Pyramid had also been affected b the Korean War and was experiencing financial problem Tri-ang therefore purchased Pyramid Toys.

By buying out both Rovex (including Zenith) an Pyramid Toys, Tri-ang had a base for a model railwa system. Richard Lines was tasked with the job of overseein the production of a comprehensive 00 gauge system fo the Tri-ang Group.

The newly built factory constructed in Westwood, near Margate, Kent in the mid-1950s to cope with the rapidly expanding Tri-ang Railways. Today it is home to the Hornby Visitor Centre and is storage for main line locomotives.

Richard fortunately took this task on board with grea enthusiasm. Vanetzian was replaced by John Hefford (original from the Zenith Motor Company), who became the Genera Manager of Rovex. Building up a well-respected team from Rove and Tri-ang, at the May 1952 British Industries Fair it was possib to launch the new Tri-ang Railways system with three locomotiv (Princess and 0-6-2T from Rovex and Trackmaster, and Tr ang's own black 0-6-0 Jinty), coaches, trucks, track, points, lev crossing, station buildings, goods shed, signal box, signals an other accessories. Such was the rush to get the layout ready tha the buildings wer made of plywood no plastic; they were bui and painted by Geo Hunt, an artist wh specialised in woo carvings. Tri-ang als built a new factory i Westwood, Marga to build the ne railway system.

A pair of Tri-ang Transcontinental pantograph double-ended locomotives on Neil Smith's vintage layout.

Almost overnight, Meccano and Trix found they had a competitor with the power of a large company seriously to challenge their dominance in the post-war 00 gauge market. Richard considered Hornby Dublo a very competent competitor, but Tri-ang was big enough to compete with Dublo and Trix, neither of which realised the impact this new system would have on them.

Not only was Tri-ang a more imaginative and forward-thinking company than Meccano (Hornby Dublo), but it was also using the new material – plastic – which not only was cheaper, but could also be moulded into various colours with greater detail.

Tri-ang was able to invest heavily in the new system, which from the start was 2-rail, much more realistic than the Hornby Dublo and Trix 3-rail track. It also kept the clockwork sets in its portfolio, aimed at the younger market. These were compatible with the electric 2-rail system and benefited from owners staying with Tri-ang when upgrading to electric trains.

The Lines group was also keen to sell its system worldwide and introduced a Transcontinental system, predominantly aimed at the Canadian, South African, Australian and New Zealand market. So colourful and exciting was this range that the UK market also demanded the items, and in the 1950s this range was sold very successfully in Britain.

Tri-ang did not rest in the 1950s, producing new and colourful locomotives and rolling stock. Hornby Dublo launched the new BR livery in the 1950s, but a lack of imagination with a very limited choice of locomotives, rolling stock and accessories allowed Tri-ang to become the No.1 system by the end of the decade. The Meccano group in the 1950s suffered on all three of its toy fronts. Tri-ang competed with its trains; Mettoy's Corgi toys (1955) seriously affected Dinky Toys; and Lego, launched in 1960, began the demise of the Meccano Construction and Bayko market. Sadly, as mentioned earlier, the Meccano chairman Roland Hornby did not have the flair, imagination and business acumen of his father Frank, and the Meccano company struggled during the latter half of the 1950s.

By 1960 Tri-ang was quoted as having around 50 per cent of the 00 gauge market, with Dublo, Trix and others controlling the rest. Dublo failed to launch 2-rail sets until 1959, however, keeping 3-rail in production, and as a result, despite some excellent new plastic buildings and more realistic 2-rail rolling stock, it struggled financially running two systems. It was also unable to stem losses from other parts of the business. Sadly, the Meccano Group went into liquidation. Tri-ang then purchased it and combined the two railway systems on 1 May 1965 becoming known as Tri-ang Hornby.

TRI-ANG ACTION SETS AND ACCESSORIES

It was not surprising that Meccano failed. Tri-ang was imaginative, focused on what the market wanted and delivered it. Sadly, Meccano just watched the competition overtake them and failed to adjust their strategy to meet the demands of its market in the late 1950s and early 1960s.

Where Tri-ang eclipsed Hornby Dublo was in the play value their train sets offered. Accessories such as overhead catenary, giraffe cars, coal hopper unloading sets, log unloading wagons, fog signals and realistic bell sets all featured in the catalogue.

to give that edge when deciding which system to buy. Several engines had a Synchrosmoke unit that when running heated smoke oil to provide realistic puffs of smoke.

However, it was the action train sets that really attracted the imagination. The artwork on many of the sets was stunning and just asked to be purchased.

The Defender Set probably had the greatest play value of any train set. It contained a searchlight wagon with a real light, four missile launchers and an exploding car. This is the set I received at Christmas 1964, which was just great fun and my friends all wanted to play with it. Switch the lights off, focus the searchlight on the exploding car primed with caps, and aim the missiles (see page 5). POW WOW! What a toy!

Although the Frontiersman Set was not an action set, Tri-ang capitalised on the popularity of cowboys and Indians in the 1960s with programmes such as *Casey Jones*, *Wagon Train* and *Bonanza* on the TV screen and John Wayne and Clint Eastwood films in the cinema. Tri-ang produced a superb colourful Wild West model 'Davy Crockett' locomotive and contemporary coaches and caboose. One could then set it up with the various toy forts and figures of the day.

Slot cars were also popular in the 1960s, and did eventually cause part of the decline of the toy train market. However, in 1962 Tri-ang launched their Minic Motorways slot car system, which was roughly 00 gauge and from the beginning was linked

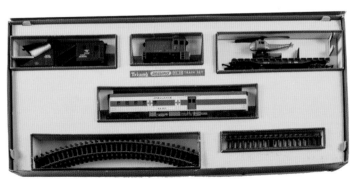

The Snow Rescue Set, with working helicopter car and a snow plough with operating blades, was copied from Lionel of America. This type of accessory had not been seen in the UK and certainly added a wow factor to Tri-ang.

The Conqueror set had a rocket launcher and exploding car. This set never made it into a Tri-ang catalogue, but it sold very well through various mail order companies such as Kay's and was another set that would give hours of fun.

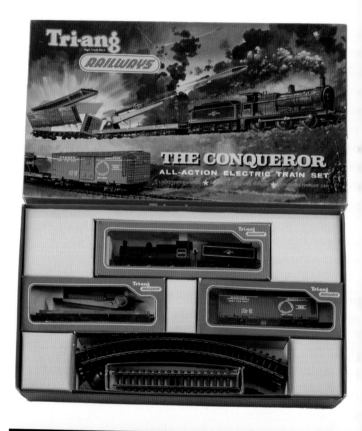

Tri-ang later named its military-style accessories Battlespace, and under Tri-ang Hornby issued the Strike Force 10 set with a catapult plane launch car and a Satellite Set with a flying satellite.

p with Tri-ang trains. Tri-ang roduced combination Minic Motorway and Tri-ang railway ets with accessories including oad rail crossing and road/rail ack. They also produced a car-oading ramp with car transporter nd a Road Railer set with the bility to move the container on oth the slot car track or the railway.

The Car-a-Belle Set with two wagons, each with six Minix cars, added another form of play value.

Tri-ang was a huge company with many subsidiaries and as able to produce other accessories to link up with their ailway system.

Young and Fogg was a rubber moulding company that Tri-ang urchased and used to produce their 'Countryside Series' of bber buildings, including a church, post office, shops, houses, rm buildings, windmill and even a small factory. It replaced the Countryside series in the early 1960s when it launched Model and, which was a pre-coloured series of plastic kits superior to irfix. Included were a church with chimes, supermarket, pylons, nd factory buildings as well as shops, houses and bungalows. It so introduced a fabulous range of factory-painted figures.

Tri-ang's Spot-On factory in Ireland made Arkitex, a plastic onstruction toy produced in 00 and 0 gauge. From each set was possible to produce significant size buildings to create

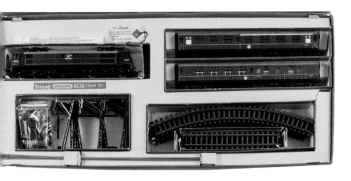

The Highwayman Set came with overhead catenary. Meccano never produced an overhead system, even though they had planned and issued an E3002 electric locomotive just before the takeover.

Tri-ang produced a superb colourful Wild West model 'Davy Crockett' locomotive and contemporary coaches and caboose. One could then set it up with the various toy forts and figures of the day. The model on the right has been repainted.

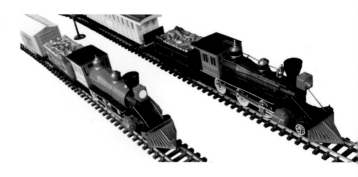

a large town or city environment. Tri-ang even produced a over-track station, which was called an Ultra Modern Station

The 00 gauge vehicle market was well provided for, b nevertheless Tri-ang produced a new range of plastic cars, va and a bus and called the series Minix. They sold them individual with various items of rolling stock, and in play packs.

TRI-ANG WRENN AND WRENN RAILWAYS

The name Wrenn has been linked with 00 gauge since 195 George and his brother Richard Wrenn (who had previous worked at Graham Farish and Victory Industries) we originally based in Lee Green, near Blackheath, South Lond and produced well-made 00 gauge 2- and 3-rail track and lat TT track, mainly for the railway modeller. They also bui various toys including boats and a slot car motor-racing syste known as Wrenn 152 that was technically very good but did n sell well due to competition from the more popular Scalextri

In January 1966 Lines Brothers, who owned Tri-an purchased a controlling interest in Wrenn to help it contin

Even older than the Wild West was Stephenson's Rocket, which came with three coaches, 'Times', 'Despatch' and 'Experience'. It was a lovely set that sold in excellent numbers.

supporting the Hornby Dublo network with the huge surplus of stock it had acquired from the Meccano factory at Binns Road. With his link up with Tri-ang, George Wrenn negotiated a deal with Tri-ang to reuse the Dublo moulds. The original moulds were then transferred to Wrenn's new factory in Basildon and from 1966 they started to produce the old Hornby 2-rail Dublo locomotives under the Wrenn and later the Tri-ang Wrenn names.

A car loading ramp with car and rail transporter, with the ability to move the car to another part of the layout by rail.

The first 'Wrenn' locomotive produced using the old Dublo moulds was 'Cardiff Castle' in 2-rail. It came with a choice of couplings, either Tri-ang tension lock or the Dublo Peco style, making the locomotive suitable for Tri-ang or Dublo 2-rail. Train sets were also sold under the Wrenn name using old Dublo stock. Wrenn sales were boosted as many of the Tri-ang Hornby catalogues from the late 1960s to early 1970s included the Wrenn range. Soon more ex-Dublo locomotives and rolling stock were reproduced.

Tri-ang Countryside Series leaflet supplement of 1960, showing the full range of rubber line-side buildings and accessories moulded by the Young and Fogg group that became part of Tri-ang.

ABOVE RIGHT
Tri-ang Arkitex Ultra Modern Station Set. A station building that could span two tracks was an excellent addition to the 1960s modern image layout.

ABOVE
A factory scene using the Tri-ang model land plastic kits. The sharp eye will notice the rare Rice Krispies wagons in the siding.

By 1971, when the Lines group itself was entering administration, George Wrenn purchased his old business back from the receiver and began to produce the Wrenn range as an independent company.

Wrenn continued to reproduce more of the old Dublo locomotives using much more imagination than Meccano with various new liveries that were attractive to the market. One of the most colourful was 'Lyme Regis' in SR green.

Although Wrenn produced ex-Dublo coaches and wagons it never produced a complete model railway system. It should

owever, be noted that after 1975 (beyond the remit of this ook) they ventured out and produced non-Dublo locomotives uch as un-rebuilt Battle of Britain, Merchant Navy and West Country streamline locomotives, Coronation class and Royal cot class locomotives as well as a very well-received Brighton Belle in both brown and cream and blue and grey. Perhaps Tri-ang should have produced this model in the early 1960s.

Wrenn continued until 1992 and its goods have been produced since then by various groups, who continue to supply models in various guises under the Wrenn name.

OPPOSITE BOTTOM
Tri-ang introduced a small but colourful range of 00 scale vehicles. Here are some examples including American issue and later playpacks.

Two early editions of Wrenn catalogue, the second showing how quick Wrenn was to introduce new liveries to the old Hornby Dublo locomotives.

EUROPEAN HO GAUGE IN BRITAIN

Despite the popularity of 00 gauge in the UK, tw companies decided to try to launch HO gauge in th UK during the 1960s and 1970s.

PLAYCRAFT

Playcraft Railways hit the UK market in 1961 with the HO gauge railway system that was produced by Jou of France. Their market strategy was to sell the mode at a very low cost and mainly through Woolworths, wh had a store in most large towns and cities and even i larger villages.

The size difference between the 00 and HO models w. quite noticeable, but Playcraft kept its prices very competiti and entered the market with both clockwork and electr train sets. The British outline models were generally qui crude, but the continental models were excellent quality ar no doubt Playcraft affected Hornby Dublo and Tri-ang sal quite hard early on.

Playcraft had a complete system, including operatir accessories such as the TPO (Travelling Post Office) se Hopper unloading set and Jouef's container trucks wi their excellent Kangourou (Road-rail) set. They even sold complete model railway that included a trackmat.

Unfortunately for Playcraft, the British market preferr 00 gauge, and eventually Playcraft called it a day and wour up their British presence in 1968.

.IMA

'he Italian manufacturer was well-known in Europe and, ke Playcraft, decided to enter the British market. In 1973 ey introduced their UK outline HO gauge locomotives and olling stock with buildings and accessories. Although their ritish range was more realistic than Playcraft it was not a access, and by 1976 it had given up with HO and launched 0 gauge. Lima eventually built up a good reputation for uality diesel locomotives, ultimately becoming part of the Iornby empire in 2004.

Low-cost Playcraft HO Railways 'Complete Train Sets' were issued with either a goods train or passenger train, and for a while affected the sales of Tri-ang.

Tri-ang HORNBY

Inter-City

Electric Train-Electric Locomotive with Pantograph and 3 Passenger Coaches.

Tri-ang HORNBY   inter ☆ city EXPRESS

R645   Tri-ang HORNBY   Freightliner

Freightliners Limited   Freightliners Limited   Freightliners Limited   Freightliners Limited   Freightliners Limited

Tri-ang HORNBY   Freightline

Electric Train-Diesel Locomotive and 3 Freightliner Trucks

TRI-ANG HORNBY AND HORNBY RAILWAYS 1965–75

TRI-ANG HORNBY

The amalgamation of these two large 00 gauge systems should have been a more equal mix of each system. The compatibility was really no problem and Hornby Dublo had some excellent rolling stock and accessories that could have formed a lasting part of the new combined system.

The amalgamation leaflet features many Hornby Dublo items. When Richard Lines first planned the takeover, it was his intention to keep Meccano producing Dublo trains in the Binns Road factory. However, the reception they received from Meccano and their general reluctance to build a working relationship forced Richard to close Dublo production and transfer all the production of 00 trains to Tri-ang's modern Margate factory.

Tri-ang Hornby was initially very successful. The new system was popular and sold in the ex-Meccano-contracted shops as well as the shops already selling Tri-ang. There was very little competition from other 00 gauge manufacturers, as Playcraft was cheap and cheerful and was mainly restricted to Woolworths, and Trix, although now producing some excellent models, did not have the same foothold in the market.

Tri-ang Hornby initially continued with the ex-Hornby Dublo stock and buildings, but passed over the locomotive moulds to Wrenn and despite the quality of the ex-Dublo buildings it was too expensive to produce them in the Tri-ang factory. The ex-Dublo buildings were all dropped by 1970, and Tri-ang

OPPOSITE
In the late 1960s Inter-City and Freightliner were the big happening on the railways, and Tri-ang came out with these two eye-catching sets.

The annual Tri-ang catalogue, now incorporating both Hornby and Minic Motorway, with a traditional Terrence Cuneo painting on the front.

Hornby introduced a new canopy station that, although not as attractive or impressive as the Dublo station, was much cheaper to produce and fitted the original Tri-ang platforms.

In 1970 System 6 track replaced Super 4, which was beginning to look dated, but unfortunately they did not take on the Dublo 2-rail track, which was more realistic than Super 4 and as good as System 6. Possibly one of the main reasons Tri-ang Hornby did not adopt the Dublo track was due to the number of clip-fit accessories for Super 4 that would have required new fittings.

Sadly, by the late 1960s and early 1970s the UK toy market was having a terrible time, getting hit by huge quantities of cheap plastic toys, many being exact copies of British toys from Hong Kong, and tin and plastic toys from Japan, as well as increasing imports from the rich toy manufacturers in the United States. The UK economy was in turmoil, with high interest rates and employee action as strikes in many engineering firms resulted in higher labour costs.

Unfortunately, even the giant Lines group could not survive, possibly because it had too many manufacturing

The Bourton-on-the-Water Model Railway is very much worth a visit and you can still see the 'new' Tri-ang Hornby canopy station in an excellent setting.

lants, almost 40. It also lost too much money in Europe, particularly ventures in France, Italy and Germany. Canada never made a profit due to the proximity of the US market, which created an oversupply. Therefore, in 1971 the Lines group was sold off to several eager buyers who took on the various parts of the business. Rovex Tri-ang-Hornby was purchased by DCM (Dunbee Combex Marx), who continued with production at Margate.

HORNBY RAILWAYS 1972-75

The first action DCM took was to rename the system Hornby Railways, as they believed Hornby was a more iconic name and would be better taking them forward. Business therefore carried on as normal and DCM did their best to add some spark into their new acquisition. Unfortunately, trains were no longer the flavour of the day. Steam trains had ceased on mainline British Railways in 1968, diesels did not have the same attraction, and by the early 1970s other toys such as Action Man, Lego, slot cars and a whole host of American toys that were heavily advertised on TV knocked the toy train market.

Hornby continued to upgrade, and introduced new liveries and locomotives, including their silver seal steam locomotives launched in 1973. However, their sales were declining and they were struggling, and even started to import cheaper European building kits such as Pola to keep costs down.

Although the annual catalogue was still eagerly awaited, it did not have the excitement the 1950s and 60s ones generated.

After the collapse of the Lines group who owned Tri-ang Hornby Railways, it was acquired and renamed Hornby Railways. Here is the first catalogue in the Hornby name, with another wonderful Terrance Cuneo painting.

BEYOND 1975

Nick Gilman's vintage Tri-ang 'Windmill Hill' layout is exhibited at toy and model railway shows around the country. Spot the Tri-ang 'Jinty' locomotive and trucks, rubber buildings and station, Dublo Dinky vehicles, Merit station staff, platform accessories and trees, Budgie 00 vehicles, Master Models telephone boxes, Lilliput and Matchbox vehicles.

THE 00 GAUGE TOY industry did not cease in 1975. However over the next few years manufacturers such as Lima from Italy became a strong competitor to Hornby. Other companies followed Airfix into the market including Mainline, Replica and Bachmann who used the Airfix moulds after they collapsed, and even Hornby today are producing trains from the original Airfix moulds.

Today the main 00 gauge companies in the UK market are Bachmann and Hornby, who between them own most of the original European toy train companies. Manufacturing is mainly in China, producing well-detailed, often hand-finished locomotives and rolling stock under a variety of names including Lima, Rivarossi, Electrotren, Heljan and many others.

So who is buying the trains now? Well, it has totally changed. The recipients of the train sets and accessories in the 1950s and 1960s were generally boys from the age of 8 to 15. Today the market is predominantly adult, in many cases the boys of the 1950s and 1960s who are still playing trains today!

Model railways have become a much smaller and more sophisticated hobby with digital control. It is still a wonderful pastime whether you play with the original toys of the 50s and 60s or the new digital 00 gauge trains of today.

APPENDIX I: ACCESSORY MANUFACTURERS 1935–75

Most of the manufacturers of railway systems such as Trix, Hornby Dublo, Tri-ang and Playcraft produced complete system with track, stations, goods depots and ineside accessories. However, a few companies specialised in accessories only and achieved excellent sales and a good reputation. Many of these companies sold their items through small toy shops, stationery and cycle shops that had toy sections, as well as corner shops and post offices, and items were often purchased with weekly pocket money.

Below are details of the main companies that produced accessories generally aimed at the 00 gauge toy train market.

Master Models produced a huge collection of metal accessories from figures to platform kiosks. The variety of accessories was astounding and most layouts in the 1950s would have been adorned with something from their vast range. Under the Wardie label they produced wooden stations, signal boxes and goods depots with the name 'Woodside'.

Crescent was set up in the early 1920s and is well known for its lead and plastic figures and animals, die-cast vehicles and other toys. In 00 gauge Crescent established a great position in producing

Master Models by Wardie produced many catalogues to show its extensive range of accessories and buildings for both 00 and TT gauge.

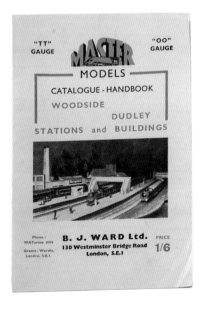

Crescent signals were hugely popular. Here is a signal gantry together with a late Brimtoy SR-style plastic footbridge.

Kitmaster catalogue showing the very popular Pullman cars, including a kitchen car that was often sought by those with a Tri-ang set that lacked the kitchen car.

signals. Almost ever boy's train set in th 1960s would have ha examples of Crescen signals, no doub sold in local corne shops and small to shops; their salesme must have been ver successful. Crescent also built an excellent 00 gauge metal S green footbridge that was later available in plastic.

Merit produced by J&L Randall of Potters Bar was probabl one of the biggest suppliers of plastic ready-made 00 gaug accessories in the 1960s and 1970s. Presented in colourf boxes, just about everything that was found on the station an goods depot as well as line-side buildings was available. No called Modelscene and owned by Peco, they still produce vast array of accessories for today's model railway.

Peco was founded by Sidney Pritchard, one of the mo influential people in the early model railway industry. produced high-quality track in all gauges with points an accessories, aimed mainly at the railway modeller. Many wh started with a toy train set moved on to Peco to produce a scen model railway. As mentioned above, Peco now owns Merit an continues to produce most of the items available in the 1960 as well as producing the excellent *Railway Modeller* magazine

Airfix used colourful packaging to sell its excellent range of plastic accessories.

Kitmaster was part of the Rosebud empire and produced excellent 00 gauge plastic kits from 1959 to 1962. These easy-to-make and well-detailed kits were a great addition to train sets of the late 1950s. Spanning the whole generation of railways, they made models from Stephenson's Rocket to the last steam locomotive built for BR, 'Evening Star'. They also produced the famous Blue Pullman train, including the kitchen car. Kitmaster also produced motorised chassis and vans to electrify the trains. BR maroon and green coaches were also successfully sold in pairs and were much cheaper than the RTR examples.

Airfix started in 1939 but it was not until 1949 they produced their first plastic kit, a Ferguson TE20 tractor. Soon they were producing aircraft, ships, cars, famous people and other kits, all of which were sold through Woolworths as well as toy shops and local post offices and newsagents. In 1962 Airfix also purchased the Kitmaster moulds when Rosebud had financial difficulties. By the mid-1960s they had a full range of model railway locomotives, rolling stock, stations, engine sheds and town buildings.

Perfect for birthday and Christmas presents, Airfix kits were one of the most popular toys of the 1960s, and every 00 gauge layout would have been complemented by Airfix accessories.

An advert for the Britains' Lilliput series that produced farm, army and civilian models in 00 gauge.

Matchbox Lesney produced hundreds of vehicles suitable for 00 gauge. Here is one of their excellent commercial truck gift sets.

Even today the original Airfix moulds are still being used, and most of the railway kits are available under the name Dapol.

Britains was one of the world's greatest model soldier and army vehicles manufacturers as well as producing farm and zoo animals, mostly to a 1:43 scale, which suited 0 gauge. However, they marketed 00 gauge figures and farm equipment through Lilliput World, and also produced 00 gauge cars and commercial vehicles including army vehicles.

Lesney Matchbox toys are world famous. Although not made to a constant scale, many of the early 1950s and 1960s 1:75 series were perfect for 00 gauge and provided excellent addition to the 00 gauge layout.

In the 1960s, **Lego** produced a superb range of HO/00 gauge vehicles including British, German and French cars, vans, VW buses, lorries and trailers, Shell and ESSO tankers and articulated Philips and Interfrigo transport lorries. It was a range that would have been perfect

for any 00 gauge railway. Sadly the range did not last into the 1970s, but these excellent models can still be found today and would not look out of place on a modern layout. Lego even produced a set of traffic policemen, cyclists, scooters and motorbikes.

Other die-cast vehicle manufactures included Morestone and Benbros. Both British manufacturers also produced 00 scale cars, as did Budgie. **Corgi** toys also issued their Husky range, which had many 00 gauge models.

In 1960 Lego launched in the UK and for the first few years produced a superb range of factory-made 00/HO scale vehicles, including British cars and commercials.

Corgi introduced the Husky range to compete with Matchbox. Their series was mainly 00 gauge and sold generally by Woolworths.

APPENDIX II: RETAILERS

Gamages produced the most extensive combined model railway, toy cars and model catalogue in the 1950s and 1960s.

G AMAGES WAS A famous London store based in Holbor that sold 00 gauge in large quantities. It also markete many toys under its own label, including Rovex and Tri-an sets. Each Christmas they had a vast 00 gauge railway buil on their toy train level. Gamages also produced an annua catalogue, which included every British manufacturer of trai sets and accessories.

Beatties was founded by Colonel S.N. Beattie as th Southgate Model shop and was very active selling Tri-ang an

Hornby Dublo during the 1960s and 1970s. It ventured on to other model areas such as slot cars and die-cast models and later video games as interest in model railways reduced. Although it expanded to 60 stores, it sadly went into administration in 2001. Some stores were taken over by Modelzone, which also went into administration in 2013.

Hamleys, as mentioned earlier, was owned by Tri-ang and was a must for every child who visited London in the 1950s and 1960s, particularly at Christmas. The shop also had a large model railway each Christmas and sold trains worldwide.

The iconic frontage of Hamleys in Regent Street, the most famous toy shop in the world, once owned by Tri-ang.

APPENDIX III: BERTRAM OTTO

Bertram Otto's model railways were magnificent exhibitions. Here is an early shot of the original model railway at Beaulieu Motor Museum.

N O BOOK ON 00 gauge toy trains would be complete without the mention of Bertram Otto. He was a children's entertainer with magic, Punch and Judy and talent contests as part of his act. From the 1950s to the early 1970s he was also responsible for some of the greatest 00/HO gauge public exhibition layouts.

Permanent model railway exhibitions were popular at seaside and other tourist attractions and Bertram was

responsible for the most well known. Using 'The World's' as a title, followed by either 'Greatest', 'Largest' or 'Finest', he created layouts at Eastbourne Winter Gardens, Olympia (1963/4), Beaulieu Motor Museum, Colchester Zoo, New York's Fair (1965), Connecticut, Scarborough Exhibition Hall, Gamages (1969/70) and other places.

The layouts were generally very large, some over 150 feet long; the New York exhibition covered 2,800 square feet! The central theme to most layouts was areas that depicted England, France, Germany and Switzerland, the City of the Future and and the ocean. All layouts had mountains with cable cars.

Locomotives and rolling stock were mainly from three manufacturers, Tri-ang Hornby, Fleischmann and British Trix. However, when one views the information booklets, one can spot Hornby Dublo and Schuco Monorails as well as Airfix kits. London's Big Ben and Paris's Eiffel Tower would be seen

This early 1970s shot of the Mevagissey Model Railway shows a Tri-ang 'Lord of the Isles' locomotive and clerestory coaches and Trix Western Diesel and even today there are some scenes including buildings from the 1970s.

A collection of early 1950s Hornby Dublo aluminium station buildings and signal box that eventually replaced the post-war wooden buildings.

The colourful headers from Airfix sets, showing the variety of accessories available at low cost and sold at every shop with a toy section from Woolworths to the local post office.

in all the layouts, together with operating features such as fountains, lights and smoke.

Most model railway exhibitions in seaside towns have now closed, and today there are very few surviving. One that has survived is the Mevagissey Model Railway, which started in 1971. It is similar to the Otto layouts and is always worth a visit. You can even spot some 1960s Tri-ang buildings on the layout.

These and the other permanent exhibition layouts gave many the inspiration to have a train set and build their own, albeit smaller, layouts.

PLACES TO VISIT

Mevagissey Model Railway, Meadow Street, Mevagissey PL26 6UL. Telephone: 01726 842457. Website: www.model-railway.co.uk

Bourton Model Railway, High Street, Bourton-on-the-Water, Cheltenham GL54 2AN. Telephone: 01451 820686. Website: www.bourtonmodelrailway.co.uk

Brighton Toy and Model Museum, 52–55 Trafalgar Street, Brighton BN1 4EB. Telephone: 01273 749494. Website: www.brightontoymuseum.co.uk

Treasured Toys, Beale Park, Lower Basildon, Pangbourne, Berkshire RG8 9NW. Website: www.bealepark.org.uk/attractions/treasured-toys

Pecorama, Underleys, Beer, Seaton EX12 3NA. Telephone: 01297 21542. Website: www.pecorama.co.uk

Wroxham Miniature World, Station Business Park, Horning Road West, Hoveton, Norwich NR12 8QJ. Telephone: 01603 781728. Website: www.wroxhamminiatureworlds.co.uk

Hornby Visitor Centre, Westwood Industrial Estate, Margate CT9 4JX. Telephone: 01843 233524 Website: www.hornby.com/uk-en/hornby-visitor-centre

Fort Victoria Model Railway, Fort Victoria, Westhill Lane, Freshwater, Yarmouth PO41 0RR. Telephone: 01983 761553. Website: www.fortvictoriamodelrailway.co.uk

Watercress Line, The Railway Station, Station Road, New Alresford SO24 9JG. Telephone: 01962 733810 Website: www.watercressline.co.uk

Bluebell Railway, Sheffield Park Station, East Sussex, TN22 3QL. Telephone: 01825 720800 Website: www.bluebell-railway.co.uk

Swanage Railway, Station House, Swanage, Dorset BH19 1HB. Telephone: 01929 425800. Website: www.swanagerailway.co.uk

House on the Hill Toy Museum, Castle Visitor Centre, Lower Street, Stansted Mountfitchet CM24 8SP. Telephone: 01279 813237. Website: www.stanstedtoymuseum.com

The Miniature World of Model Railways, Ormesby Hall, Ladgate Lane, Ormesby, Middlesbrough TS3 0SR. Telephone: 01642 324188. Website: www.nationaltrust.org.uk/ormesby-hall

Devon Railway Centre, Bickleigh, Tiverton EX16 8RG. Telephone: 01884 855671. Website: www.devonrailwaycentre.co.uk

Model Railway, Telford Steam Railway, The Old Loco Shed, Bridge Rd, Horsehay, Telford, Shropshire TF4 3UH. Telephone: 01952 503880. Website: telfordsteamrailway.co.uk

The Model Railway Exhibition, New Romney Station, New Romney, Kent TN28 8PL. Telephone: 01797 362 353. Website: www.rhdr.org.uk/model-railway-exhibition

Polperro Model Village, Mill Hill, Polperro, Looe PL13 2RP. Telephone: 01503 272378. Website: www.polperromodelvillage.co.uk

Bekonscot Model Village, Warwick Road, Beaconsfield HP9 2PL. Telephone: 01494 672919. Website: www.bekonscot.co.uk

National Railway Museum, Leeman Road, York YO26 4XJ. Telephone: 03330 161 010. Website: www.railwaymuseum.org.uk

Museum of Childhood, Cambridge Heath Road, London E2 9PA. Telephone: 020 8983 5200. Website: www.vam.ac.uk/moc

Todmorden Toy and Model Museum, 13 Rochdale Road, Todmorden OL14 5AA. Telephone: 01706 818365. Website: www.visitcalderdale.com/attra-todmorden-toy-model-museum

Milestones Museum, Basingstoke Leisure Park, Churchill Way West, Basingstoke RG22 6PG. Telephone: 01256 639550. Website: www.milestonesmuseum.org.uk

FURTHER READING

Angell, Dave. *Tri-ang Collectables*. Amberley, 2017

Brookes, Paul. *The Illustrated History of Hugar*. Paul Brookes, 2014

Brookes, Paul. *The Illustrated Kemlows Story: Including the Mastermodel Story*. Paul Brookes, 2009

Brown, Kenneth. *The British Toy Industry*. Shire, 2011

Carlson, Pierce. *Toy Trains: A History*. Gollancz, 1986

Foster, Michael, and Michael Bowes. *British Toy Trains*. 5 volumes.

Foster, Michael. *Hornby Dublo Trains*. New Cavendish, 1987

Fuller, Roland, and Allen Levy. *The Bassett-Lowke Story*. New Cavendish, 1982

Hammond, Pat. *Tri-ang Railways: The Story of Rovex, Vol. 1: 1950–65*. New Cavendish, 1999

Hammond, Pat. *Tri-Ang Hornby: The Story of Rovex, Vol. 2: 1965–1971*. New Cavendish, 1999

Hammond, Pat. *Tri-Ang: The Story of Rovex, Vol. 3: 1972–1996 (Hornby Railways)*. New Cavendish, 1999)

Knight, Stephen. *Let's Stick Together*. Irwell Press, 1998

Marsh, Hugo, and Pierce Carlson. *Christie's Toy Trains*. Watson-Guptill Publications, 2002

Matthewman, Tony. *The History of Trix Railways in Britain*. New Cavendish, 1994

Randall, Peter. *Recent Locomotives, 1947–70 (Troy Model Club)*. Thomas Nelson and Sons, 1970)

Tri-ang Railways: The First Ten Years. Rovex, 1962

Salter, Brian. *The Ultimate Book of Spot-On Models*. InHouse Publications, 2013

Salter, Brian. *Model Towns and Villages*, In House Publications, 2014

Salter, Brian. *Building Toys*. Shire, 2011

INDEX